Lerner SPORTS

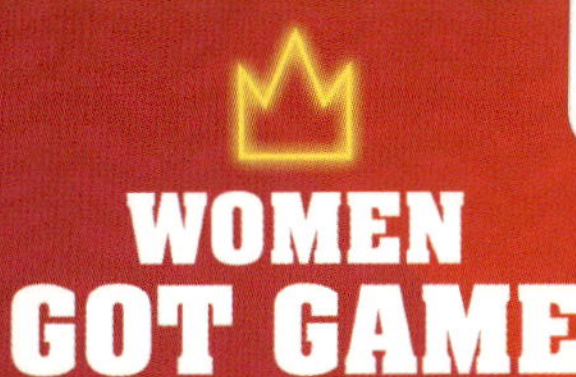

WOMEN GOT GAME

WOMEN'S PROFESSIONAL BASKETBALL

MEL HAMMOND

Lerner Publications ◆ Minneapolis

Lerner Publications Company
An imprint of Lerner Publishing Group, Inc.
241 First Avenue North
Minneapolis, MN 55401 USA

For reading levels and more information, look up this title at www.lernerbooks.com.

Main body text set in Aptifer Slab LT Pro.
Typeface provided by Linotype AG.

Editor: Evan Villas **Designer:** Mary Ross
Lerner team: Sue Marquis

Library of Congress Cataloging-in-Publication Data

Names: Hammond, Mel, author.
Title: Women's professional basketball / Mel Hammond.
Description: Minneapolis, MN : Lerner Publications, 2025. | Series: Women got game (lerner sports) | Includes bibliographical references and index. | Audience: Ages 7–11 | Audience: Grades 2–3 | Summary: "*Swish!* Women have been playing basketball for more than 130 years. Young readers will explore the history of women's professional basketball through its exhilarating moments, nail-biting championships, and spectacular athletes"— Provided by publisher.
Identifiers: LCCN 2024039732 (print) | LCCN 2024039733 (ebook) | ISBN 9798765668894 (library binding) | ISBN 9798765683590 (paperback) | ISBN 9798765682333 (epub)
Subjects: LCSH: Basketball for women—Juvenile literature. | Women basketball players—Juvenile literature. | Basketball—Juvenile literature.
Classification: LCC GV886 .H26 2025 (print) | LCC GV886 (ebook) | DDC 796.323082—dc23/eng/20240909

LC record available at https://lccn.loc.gov/2024039732
LC ebook record available at https://lccn.loc.gov/2024039733

Manufactured in the United States of America
1-1011985-53860-1/17/2025

TABLE OF CONTENTS

BATTLE AGAINST THE BUZZER

On October 18, 2023, the New York Liberty faced the Las Vegas Aces in Game 4 of the Women's National Basketball Association (WNBA) Finals. Every dribble, every pass, and every shot would count. Who would take home the trophy?

The Liberty started strong. Point guard Courtney Vandersloot led the team to a nine-point lead by halftime. Two of the Aces players had injuries and were unable to play. But superstar center A'ja Wilson wasn't going home without a fight.

In the third quarter, Wilson scored point after point. The Aces pulled ahead by two. It all came down to the fourth quarter.

FAST FACTS

- THE WNBA WAS FOUNDED ON APRIL 24, 1996.
- SHERYL SWOOPES WAS THE FIRST PLAYER TO JOIN THE WNBA.
- LISA LESLIE WAS THE FIRST PLAYER TO SLAM DUNK DURING A WNBA GAME.
- THE LOS ANGELES SPARKS WON THE LAST GAME OF THE 2016 FINALS BY A SINGLE POINT.

Fans held their breath during the final minutes of the game. The lead went back and forth. With 41 seconds to go, the Aces pulled ahead by one. Could the Liberty regain the lead?

With only 8.8 seconds remaining in the game, Vandersloot saw her chance. She caught a pass, took her shot, and—missed! The buzzer sounded. The game was over!

The Aces erupted in cheers. They had won 70–69! They became the first WNBA team to win back-to-back championships in 21 years.

The history of the WNBA is full of heart-pounding moments like this. Get ready to be dunked into the incredible world of women's pro basketball!

The Las Vegas Aces celebrate with the 2023 WNBA Finals trophy.

Courtney Vandersloot passes the ball during Game 4 of the WNBA Finals.

Chapter 1

MAKING HISTORY

Students at the University of Wisconsin–Madison playing basketball in 1900

In 1891, physical education teacher James Naismith invented the game of basketball. At the time, many people thought women shouldn't play sports. But college gym teacher Senda Berenson thought differently. In 1893, she taught her female students to play basketball as a fun way to exercise.

The path for most women to play basketball was not easy. It was even harder for women of color. When athletes of color were not allowed to join the same teams as white players, they formed their own teams. One of these teams was the Fort Shaw Indian School Girls Basketball Team. These ten Native American women played at the 1904 World's Fair. They beat every other team.

Members of the Fort Shaw Indian School Girls Basketball Team

EARLY DAYS

Early basketball looked different than it does today. For hoops, players used fruit baskets. Dribbling wasn't allowed.

The years 1904 to 1950 were known as the Black Fives Era. This is because many all-Black basketball teams formed during this time. The teams were called Black Fives because each team had five players on the court at a time. The first recorded game between two all-Black women's teams happened in 1910. The New York Girls beat the Jersey Girls 12–3.

For a long time, most public schools only let boys play basketball. But things changed in 1972. A law called Title IX said that school sports must be open to everyone. It gave many more girls the chance to play basketball.

A player looks to pass during the 1986 State Championship Tournament in Texas.

During the 1970s and 1980s, the sport became much more popular. Women's basketball was added to the Olympics in 1976. Team USA brought home the silver medal. Soon after, the National Collegiate Athletic Association started supporting women's basketball. That meant women could finally play basketball in college.

A group of kids play basketball during the 1980s.

Players fight for a rebound during a game in the short-lived Women's Professional Basketball League.

Although the men's National Basketball Association had formed in 1949, there was no pro league for women. The Women's Professional Basketball League was created in 1978. But it only lasted three seasons.

Players from the New York Liberty and Los Angeles Sparks in action during the first ever WNBA game in 1997

Things changed on April 24, 1996, when the WNBA was founded. The league started with eight teams. Its first game took place in 1997 between the New York Liberty and the Los Angeles Sparks. About 14,000 fans cheered in the stands. Finally, women could become pro basketball players.

Trish Roberts (*right*) battles against two defenders during the 1976 Olympics.

Chapter 2

BALLER MOMENTS

Kym Hampton (*left*) of the New York Liberty makes a jump shot during the 1999 WNBA Finals.

Basketball is an action-packed sport. Since the WNBA began, it has been full of exciting moments. In the 1999 WNBA Finals, the New York Liberty were neck and neck with the best team in the league, the Houston Comets.

With only 2.4 seconds remaining in the game, Comets forward Tina Thompson made a basket. The Comets were now ahead by two points. Their fans roared. Everyone thought the game was over.

But Liberty point guard Teresa Weatherspoon hadn't given up. She stood 50 feet (15 m) from the basket—a nearly impossible shot. She launched the ball across the court. *Swish!* The ball sunk into the net. No one could believe it. The Liberty had won the game!

Teresa Weatherspoon (*right*) sizes up her defender during Game 2 of the 1999 WNBA Finals.

A couple of great WNBA moments happened in 2002. The Los Angeles Sparks were playing the Miami Sol. Sparks center Lisa Leslie caught the ball. She broke away from the other players.

The crowd held its breath as Leslie approached the basket. She jumped into the air. Her hand slammed the ball through the net. Leslie had just made the first slam dunk in WNBA history.

Since then, eight other WNBA players have dunked during games. Brittney Griner holds the record. She's dunked 26 times.

Lisa Leslie reaches up to make the first dunk in WNBA history.

Cheryl Ford (*right*) takes a shot during Game 2 of the 2003 WNBA Finals.

The Detroit Shock had played poorly in the 2002 season. They had the worst record in the WNBA. Most fans didn't have much hope for this underdog team. But in 2003, the Shock proved doubters wrong.

New players joined the roster, including star rookie Cheryl Ford. They hired a new coach. Finally, the Shock found their groove. They climbed to the number one spot in the league. But the 2003 Finals would be the team's true test.

In 2003, only two teams had ever won a WNBA championship: the Los Angeles Sparks and the Houston Comets. But when the Shock hit the court in the Finals, they dominated. After losing to the Sparks in the first game in the series, the Shock regrouped to win the next two. They took home the 2003 Finals trophy! It was the first time any American pro team had climbed from last place to a championship win in one year.

Swin Cash of the Detroit Shock celebrates after winning the 2003 WNBA Finals.

Candace Parker (*left*) of the Sparks jumps to grab a rebound during Game 5 of the 2016 WNBA Finals.

The Minnesota Lynx faced the Sparks in Game 5 of the 2016 Finals. In the fourth quarter, the teams were tied 73–73. Rebekkah Brunson made a free throw for the Lynx. Candace Parker then scored for the Sparks. Maya Moore grabbed a point for the Lynx. It was back-and-forth. It could be anyone's game.

Nneka Ogwumike takes the game-winning shot during Game 4 of the 2016 WNBA Finals.

With 9.4 seconds left in the fourth quarter, the Lynx were one point ahead. Sparks forward Nneka Ogwumike took a shot. But Lynx center Sylvia Fowles swatted it out of the air. There were only 3.1 seconds left when Ogwumike tried one more time. This time, the ball fell through the net. The Sparks won the 2016 Finals by a single point!

ALL EYES ON CLARK

Before joining the WNBA in 2024, Caitlin Clark was one of the best college basketball players. She played for the University of Iowa. In her four seasons with the team, she scored more points, 3,951, than any college player in history.

Caitlin Clark is a point guard for the Indiana Fever. In July 2024, she broke the WNBA record for assists in a single game. She made 19. That season, a Fever versus Chicago Sky game became the most watched WNBA game in 23 years. Over two million fans watched.

Chapter 3

HOOP HEROES

Sheryl Swoopes poses with her third WNBA Most Valuable Player award in 2005.

In 1997, Sheryl Swoopes became the first player to join the WNBA. She helped the Comets win four WNBA championships in a row in 1997, 1998, 1999, and 2000. She was also named Most Valuable Player (MVP) in 2000, 2002, and 2005.

Sue Bird is one of the best point guards in history. She holds the record for most career assists with 3,234. She's also the only WNBA player to win championships in three different decades.

Diana Taurasi is famous for her long, steady career. She's the league's all-time leading scorer. Over her 20-year career, she's scored over 10,000 points for the Phoenix Mercury.

Diana Taurasi shoots a free throw during the 2010 WNBA playoffs.

SWOOPES SHOES

Sheryl Swoopes was the first women's basketball player with shoes that fans could buy. The Nike Air Swoopes hit stores in 1995, just months before the WNBA was founded.

Maya Moore was known for helping her team win. The Minnesota Lynx earned four WNBA titles with Moore on the team. Moore is also a champion off the court. In 2019, she retired from basketball to become an activist. She helps people who have been wrongly charged with crimes.

After a great first season in 2018, A'ja Wilson was named Rookie of the Year. She's one of the best players in the league. She led the Las Vegas Aces to back-to-back championships in 2022 and 2023. In 2024, she set a WNBA record for scoring at least 20 points for 20 games in a row.

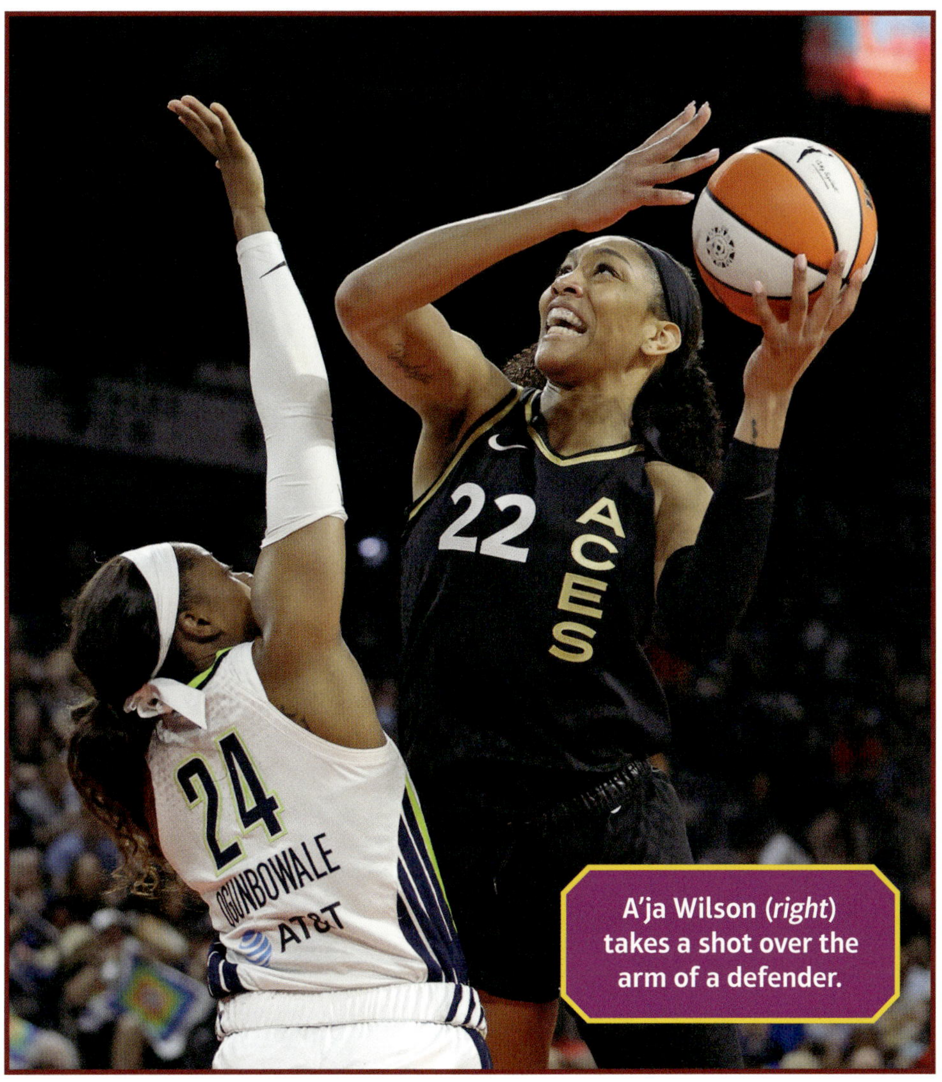

A'ja Wilson (*right*) takes a shot over the arm of a defender.

Sabrina Ionescu is known for shooting three-pointers. In 2023, she broke the WNBA and NBA records for scoring the most points in a three-point contest. Ionescu scored 37 points out of a possible 40. That means she made more than 92 percent of her shots!

The WNBA is home to many amazing athletes. It's no wonder more and more fans are tuning in to watch games each season. The league continues to inspire young women to play this exciting game. Who will be the next champion?

Sabrina Ionescu shoots a three-pointer during a 2024 game against the Phoenix Mercury.

Maya Moore (*center*) celebrates the Minnesota Lynx winning the 2013 WNBA Finals.

GLOSSARY

activist: a person who fights for a cause

center: a player who usually stays close to the basket and in the middle of the court

forward: a player who usually plays near the basket

found: to start something

free throw: an open shot taken from behind a set line after a foul by an opponent

guard: a player stationed in the backcourt

quarter: a 10-minute period of a WNBA game. Each game has four quarters.

rookie: a first-year player

roster: a list of players on a team

slam dunk: a shot made by jumping high into the air and throwing the ball down through the basket

three-pointer: a shot made from behind the three-point line, worth three points

underdog: a team that isn't expected to win

LEARN MORE

Hoehn, Jim. *WNBA*. Minneapolis: Essential Library, 2021.

Rajczak, Nelson. *Caitlin Clark: College Basketball GOAT*. Buffalo: Gareth Stevens, 2025.

Smith, Elliott. *Hoops Heroes: The Untold Story of Black Basketball*. Minneapolis: Lerner Publications, 2025.

Sports Illustrated: WNBA
https://www.si.com/wnba

WNBA
https://www.wnba.com

Women's Basketball Hall of Fame
https://wbhof.com

INDEX

PHOTO ACKNOWLEDGMENTS

Image credits: Bruce Bennett/Getty Images, p. 4; Sarah Stier/Getty Images, pp. 6, 7; Blanchard Harper/Wisconsin Historical Society/Getty Images, p. 8; History and Art Collection/Alamy Stock Photo, p. 9; Bob Daemmrich/Alamy Stock Photo, p. 11; H. Armstrong Roberts/ClassicStock/Getty Images, p. 12; Steve Campbell/Houston Chronicle via Getty Images, p. 13; Brian Bahr/Allsport via Gettty Images, p. 14; Walter Iooss Jr./Sports Illustrated via Getty Images, p. 15; Todd Warshaw/Allsport via Getty Images, pp. 16, 17; Lisa Blumenfeld/NBAE/Getty Images, p. 18; Tom Pidgeon/Getty Images, p. 19; AP Photo/Paul Warner, p. 20; Hannah Foslien/Getty Images, pp. 21, 22; Gregory Shamus/Getty Images, p. 23; AP Photo/Steve Yeater, p. 24; Christian Petersen/Getty Images, pp. 25, 28; Ethan Miller/Getty Images, p. 27; Kevin C. Cox/Getty Images, p. 29.

Design elements: Vect0r0vich/Getty Images; sarayut Thaneerat/Getty Images.

Cover: Steve Marcus/Las Vegas Sun via AP (top); AP Photo/Abbie Parr (bottom).